Quick Quilts
Across the Curriculum

A Patchwork of Delightful No-Sew Quilting Projects and Activities to Showcase Students' Learning in Math, Social Studies, Language Arts, and More

by Kathy Pike, Jean Mumper, and Alice Fiske

We'll piece together a wonderful year!

SCHOLASTIC
PROFESSIONAL BOOKS

NEW YORK • TORONTO • LONDON • AUCKLAND • SYDNEY
MEXICO CITY • NEW DELHI • HONG KONG • BUENOS AIRES

To everyone whose PIECE is important
in the education of a child

ACKNOWLEDGMENTS

We'd like to acknowledge the students at Cambridge Central School, at
Ostrander Elementary School in the Wallkill Central School District, and
Roxbury Central School District, whose work is featured in this book; the teachers
whose efforts in "piecing their students' education together" are greatly appreciated
(Therese Gilbert, Teddy Harrington, Terri Hewson, Sue McKeighan, Ilene Quackenbush,
Judy Russert, Molly Oakley, Tim Ogilive, Marjorie Ridler, and Judy Woelfersheim); and
our editors at Scholastic Inc., Liza Charlesworth and Maria Chang.

Cover and interior design by **Holly Grundon**
Edited by **Denise Rinaldo**
Interior photographs by **Kathy Pike**
Interior illustrations by **Maxie Chambliss and Jean Mumper**

ISBN: 0-439-23468-9

Contents

About This Book

America is not like a blanket—one piece of
unbroken cloth, the same color, the same
texture, the same size. America is more like
a quilt—many pieces, many sizes, all woven
and held together by a common thread.

—THE REV. JESSE JACKSON

A classroom can also be likened to a quilt—a collection of unique children, similar to the patchwork pieces in a quilt, whose efforts can be joined to create a caring and cooperative learning environment. Quilts can serve as symbols of a classroom's uniqueness and its desire to work together.

In the last decade, teachers across the United States have begun using quilting as a teaching tool. This book will show you how to bring quilting to your classroom. Most of the curricular areas covered in elementary classrooms can be presented or showcased using quilts or quilt-like projects. Quilting offers a unique means of presenting or reinforcing the information or concepts that you teach, and an additional way to have students demonstrate their knowledge. Through this book, you'll learn how to use quilting as a community builder, and see how it can become a teaching tool across the curriculum—in social studies, language arts, science, and math.

Although we briefly discuss fabric quilting in this book, most of the projects we describe are nontraditional in both format and materials. We'll show you how to make quilts from materials you've never imagined, such as plastic bags, envelopes, paper plates, and foam trays. We've designed the book to be used flexibly, and the ideas presented are meant to be springboards for the various kinds of classroom explorations that occur on a regular basis.

Using This Book

This book is divided into two main sections: The first—"How to Piece It Together"—gives basic instructions for making 14 different kinds of nontraditional quilts. The second section— "Making It Happen: Quilting Activities Across the Curriculum"—offers examples of how some of the quilting formats presented at the beginning of the book have been put into practice by real kids in real classrooms in all subject areas. Each example includes tips for how they might work in yours.

For instance, you will see in the second section how an envelope quilt was used in one class's study of endangered animals. It was a great project! But another quilting format could have been just as effective. If you happen to be teaching a unit on animals and you like the envelope quilt, by all means replicate it in your classroom.

In both sections, we provide illustrations, step-by-step instructions, and photos. But we also hope you will use this book to mix and match—the way quilters do—to create projects that are unique reflections of you and your students. Following the two main sections, you will find:

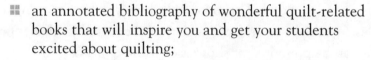
Shape
Poetry Quilt

- an annotated bibliography of wonderful quilt-related books that will inspire you and get your students excited about quilting;

- nine pages of reproducible quilt block patterns for you to use as you and your students create your own quilts. Each quilt block is divided geometrically in a different way. Depending on your quilt's theme, students can color the sections, write information inside them, or decorate them in other ways. The possibilities are truly unlimited!

Due to the very nature of the piecing and patching that is necessary when creating the quilting projects, quilting will help teach your students to be individuals (like the individual patchwork pieces) even as they work cooperatively as a class. The quilting experience enhances the learning and the atmosphere. Quilts join a class together. Happy quilting!

Quilts in History

This quilt's a piece of living history. It speaks to me in voices long passed away.

—A West Virginian quilter

Quoted in *With Needle and Thread: A Book About Quilts* by Raymond Bial
(Houghton Mifflin, 1996)

Quilting is truly an ancient art. The oldest-known quilted fabric is a garment found on a carving of an Egyptian pharaoh. The earliest-known bed quilt, dated from the 14th century, was found in Italy.

Quilting came to this continent with Europeans who crossed the Atlantic Ocean in search of a new life. It made its way west through the Appalachians and onto the prairie, where it became an absolute necessity. Fabric was costly and scarce, and quilting allowed families to patch old bedcovers together and create new ones from fabric scraps.

Before long, the quilts took on entirely new looks, and the patches on the quilts appeared to form new designs. The designs were a reflection of the early Americans' lives. Some patterns, such as Flying Geese, were inspired by nature. Others were derived from historical events such as the Westward Expansion, which inspired the Covered Wagon Trail pattern, and the Underground Railroad, which was symbolized in the Jacob's Ladder pattern.

For early Americans, quilts were far more than simple bedspreads. Autograph, album, and friendship quilts, which included the quilter's own words, signature, or special symbol, helped ease the separation from loved ones for those who crossed our country and for those who were left behind. Quilts were also used to wrap items to keep them from breaking as the pioneers crossed our country, and to cushion the hard seats on wagons. Quilts even helped soften the blow of death. Those who died on the journey west were frequently wrapped and buried in quilts.

As technology advanced and women entered the workforce, the emphasis became focused on modern products, resulting in cherished quilts being stored or given away. The interest in quilting faded.

Today, quilting is back. Album quilts, such as the AIDS Memorial Quilt, have found their place in modern times for delivering political or social messages. Quilting has become a highly respected and appreciated art form, and it is everywhere—on beds, pillows, and wall hangings. And most important for the readers of this book, quilting has made its way to the classroom! Cherish your part in this rich tradition.

Piecing It Together in the Classroom: 21st-Century Quilt Patterns

As an introduction to quilting, share with students some of the traditional quilt patterns shown here, and discuss the origins of those patterns. Then ask students what parts of their own lives could be symbolized in a quilt pattern. What is the modern equivalent of the log cabin or the journey west? Pass out paper and have students sketch designs for 21st-century quilt patterns. Display the student work on a bulletin board or use the drawings as quilt squares in one of the quilting formats presented in this book.

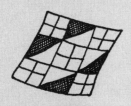

Covered Wagon Trail
Pioneer families traveled west in cloth-covered wagons packed with all of their belongings. This quilt pattern symbolizes a convoy of wagons moving across the plains. What is the modern equivalent of this journey?

Bear's Paw
Fur trappers searched the woods for bear tracks. This quilt pattern symbolizes the bear's four toes and sharp claws. What animals are of key importance in modern life?

Corn and Beans
Native Americans taught the Europeans to eat corn and beans together. It was called succotash. What foods from other cultures do you eat?

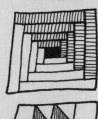

Log Cabin
Pioneers built their houses from whole logs because there were no sawmills to cut the logs into boards. This quilt pattern represents how the cabins were constructed. How do we build our homes today?

Cake Stand
The pioneers helped each other at harvest time. Once all the crops were in, they would celebrate with a feast featuring delicious cakes. This quilt pattern depicts a cake on a traditional cake stand with a pedestal. What foods do we eat at celebrations today?

How to Piece It Together:
14 Ways to Quilt in Your Classroom

We begin with paper and tape, and work up to fabric and thread. In between we show you how to make quilts from vinyl window shades and plastic bags—and even more unusual materials! Here's hoping that after you read this section, you'll never think about quilts the same way again.

Quilting Fundamentals: The Basic Quilt

The most basic quilt is made from blocks of paper decorated by students and assembled into a whole. It is simple to do, but infinitely flexible. Below are instructions for making a basic paper quilt. These instructions also apply to the creation of some of the more complex quilts. Read them before you get started.

Quilt Layout

- Regardless of the quilt format you plan to use, sketch the layout of your quilt before you start. Decide whether you want to create a nine-block quilt, a 16-block quilt, or any other combination. Number the blocks in your sketch, determine how each will be used, and decide which student or group of students will be responsible for making each block. You can have students create unique designs for each block or alternate student-designed blocks with simple blocks of color—anything you want!

- Decide whether you want to put a border and/or a heading on your quilt, then plan how they will fit in with the whole.

■ Before students start working on their blocks, share your layout sketch with them. Make sure they understand how their individual pieces will fit into the whole. This will give them a sense of purpose and classroom community.

Quilt Blocks

In most of the quilt formats and projects in this book, students begin with a quilt block. At the back of this book (beginning on p. 56), we provide nine reproducible quilt block patterns. To use them:

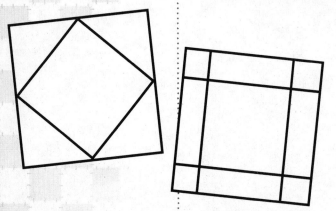

■ decide which pattern best suits your project. For example, if you are asking students to decorate their block with rhyming words, you may prefer a block that is divided into many sections. If you are asking each student to do a single illustration of a tree, a simpler block may be more appropriate.

■ photocopy as many blocks as you need (plus some extras for students who want to start over) and hand them out to students.

Quilt Backgrounds

After students have constructed their individual quilt blocks and you have planned your layout, the blocks can be joined together and displayed in a variety of ways. The simplest method is to tape or thumb-tack the paper quilt blocks to a background. The background can be totally plain or can relate to the quilt's topic. Some examples:

■ a bulletin board

■ posterboard

■ mural paper

■ newspaper

■ gift wrap related to your theme (such as animals gift wrap for a zoo quilt or construction vehicles gift wrap for a building quilt)

■ fabric related to your theme

■ wallpaper

■ a map

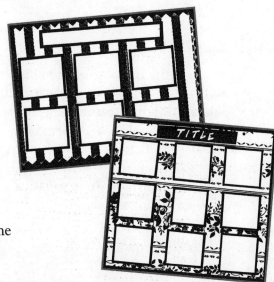

Plastic Bag Quilt

This quilting style is fabulous because it is so flexible. Zip-top plastic bags become quilt squares and can be used to hold all sorts of things. You can change the contents of the bag—and thus the nature of the quilt—quickly and easily.

Quilt It!

 1. Decide on a theme for your quilt. Then, design your quilt layout and assign each student a quilt "block" to create. The block can be anything that fits in a plastic bag—from information written on a sheet of paper to a drawing or a sculpture.

 2. Line each plastic bag with a cardboard square. This will hold the bag's shape and create a background for student work.

 3. Have students place their work—the quilt contents—into the plastic bags and zip them shut.

 4. Line up the bags in equal rows to form the quilt pattern. Attach each bag to the one next to it using clear plastic tape or colored vinyl tape.

 5. Make three-inch loops of yarn or ribbon, then tape them to the back of the top row of bags.

 6. Run a dowel rod through the loops. The dowel can be hung on hooks, suspended from strings, or secured to any surface using suction-cup hooks.

Materials

- square plastic zip-top bags of desired size (sandwich, quart, or gallon)
- cardboard squares the same size as the plastic bags
- clear plastic tape or colored vinyl tape
- yarn or ribbon
- wooden dowel rod
- suction-cup hooks

See It in Action

Olympics Quilt (p. 33); Grandma Moses Biographical Time Line Quilt (p. 36); News Quilt (p. 37); Our State Quilt (p. 37); Literature Response Quilt (p. 44); The ABCs of Rocks and Minerals Quilt (p. 50)

Other Ideas

▪ Make an alphabet plastic bag quilt using six rows of five bags. You will end up with four extra bags that can be filled with quilt blocks stating the names of the class "quilters," the date, or other key facts.

▪ A plastic bag quilt can be made for each student in the class and used to display writing, research reports, or art.

Artifact Quilt

Quilts don't have to be made from blocks created by students! You and your students can also construct quilts from actual objects or artifacts, such as photographs, postcards, menus, and maps.

Materials

▪ artifacts, such as postcards, menus, business cards, labels, book jackets, or photographs

▪ quilt background of your choosing

▪ tape, tacks, glue, or other supplies for attaching the artifacts to the background

Quilt It!

 1 Decide on a theme for your quilt. Collect appropriate artifacts and have students arrange them in a pleasing fashion.

 2 Have students attach the artifacts to the background.

 3 Captions may be placed underneath the artifacts as part of the quilt, or students can write a description of the quilt—its purpose, its contents, the "quilters," and the date it was created—to be displayed near the quilt.

See It in Action

Postcard and Map Quilt (p. 39); Foliage Photograph Quilt (p. 51); Food Label Mystery Quilt (p. 53)

Envelope Quilt

You can find envelopes in a staggering variety of sizes, shapes, colors, and designs—and they're all great for quilting! Students can also make their own envelopes (see p. 14). When used in quilting, envelopes are filled with something meaningful.
They can hold information on historical figures, animals, or types of shelters. Envelope quilts are interactive and beckon children (and adults) to look inside and learn!

Materials

- envelopes (made by students or purchased)
- quilt background of your choosing
- artifacts or information to insert into the envelopes (such as photographs, magazine articles, or student work)
- tape, tacks, glue, or other supplies for attaching envelopes to the quilt background

Quilt It!

 1   Decide on a theme for your quilt and, with students, design a quilt layout.

 2   Have students label the outside of each envelope with a topic and, if appropriate, decorate it with an illustration.

Have students create the contents of the envelope or put existing contents into the envelopes.

 Attach the envelopes to the background according to your layout.

 Encourage students to add new information or items to the envelopes for as long as the quilt is displayed.

See It in Action

Endangered Species Quilt (p. 52)

Other Idea

■ Use an envelope quilt to represent the 50 states, with an envelope for each state. Have students decorate the envelopes and fill them with key information about the state, such as a map, its state bird and state flower, and famous people from that state. Display them on a background made from a map of the United States.

Making an Envelope

Give students a square sheet of paper, a smaller piece of paper that will fit inside the envelope, and the following instructions:

1. Using a pencil, number each corner of the square from 1 to 4. Place the square in front of you, with the corner numbered 1 toward you.

2. Place the smaller piece of paper at the center of the square.

3. Take the left corner (2) and fold it over the smaller piece, forming a triangle.

4. Fold corner 4 over the smaller piece of paper. It, too, will create a triangle shape and will overlap the first fold.

5. Fold corner 1 over the two existing flaps to create the bottom of the envelope.

6. The top corner (3) can be left as is (if it is to be hung open on a bulletin board) or can be folded over to create the top of the envelope. The overlapping edges of the pieces of the envelope can be glued so that the contents will not spill out.

Foam Tray Quilt

Do you feel a little guilty when you throw away those plastic foam trays? Well, turn them into a quilt and feel guilty no more! The foam trays can be used to hold student art projects, then arranged on a background to resemble quilt blocks. (For health and safety reasons, avoid plastic foam trays that were used to pack meat.)

Quilt It!

 1 Decide on a theme for your quilt, then have students brainstorm ways to represent the theme on the foam trays. Tell students that the trays are excellent for holding three-dimensional art projects, such as small sculptures.

 2 Provide students with materials and have them complete their projects and attach them to the foam trays. Remind them that the trays will be hanging, not sitting down.

 3 Create a layout for your quilt.

 4 Attach the trays to your background. A fabric background greatly enhances the quilt-like effect. If desired, put captions beneath or beside the trays to explain what is being depicted.

See It in Action

Lighthouse Quilt (p. 35)

Materials

- plastic foam trays
- art supplies to decorate the trays, such as construction paper, bubble wrap, paint, and markers
- quilt background of your choosing
- tacks, glue, Velcro®, or other supplies for attaching the foam trays to the background

Paper Plate Quilt

nstead of using quilt blocks, why not try quilt circles? Paper plates make ideal quilt circles and, with so many decorative plates on the market today, the possibilities for creating Paper Plate Quilts are endless.

Materials

- paper plates (decorated or plain, to suit your theme)
- a quilt background of your choosing
- art supplies to decorate the paper plates
- ribbon or commercial borders
- glue, tacks, or stapler

Quilt It!

 1   Choose a theme for your quilt, then select paper plates that will work best with it. Colored or heavily designed plates work well if artwork or objects are going to be glued onto them. Plain white plates are best if students will be drawing directly on them—to make faces, for example.

 2   Work with students to come up with a layout for your quilt. Have students decorate the plates.

 3   Attach the plates to your background and use strips of ribbon to create quilt-like borders.

See It in Action

Acrostic Poetry Quilt (p. 43)

Other Ideas

- Faces (emotions, portraits of famous people, portraits of characters from literature)
- Planets and other celestial bodies
- Poetry or prose written in a spiral (beginning at the center of the plate and spiraling out)

16

Paper Frame Quilt

To add perspective and depth to a paper quilt, quilt blocks can be replaced with student-made paper frames (see p. 18) that showcase artwork, photographs, or student writing.

Materials

- paper squares
- student illustrations or photographs
- a quilt background of your choosing
- glue, tape, staples, or tacks

Quilt It!

 1 Decide on a theme for your quilt and work with students to design a layout.

 2 Give students square sheets of paper and have them make frames by following the directions on page 18. (Remember that the finished frames will be smaller than the paper you start with.)

 3 Have students make or look for artwork to be displayed in the frames.

 4 Have students insert the artwork into the frames. If you like, have them glue the frames into place.

 5 Arrange the frames according to your layout and attach them to the background.

See It in Action

Idiom Quilt (p. 41)

Other Ideas

- Self-portrait quilt for the beginning of the year
- Quilt featuring student illustrations of characters from their favorite books

Making a Frame

1. Using a pencil, mark the midpoints on each side of a square piece of paper. Then mark the center.

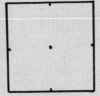

2. Fold each corner to the center point and crease the edges.

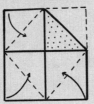

3. Take the points at the center and fold them under to reach the creased edge.

4. This creates a frame with finished edges and mitered corners.

Pellon® and Felt Quilt

Materials

- Pellon® for quilt blocks
- felt for background
- crayons or markers
- glue
- cardboard squares
- ribbon

If you want to try your hand at a fabric quilt, start with one made of felt or Pellon®. No sewing required! Felt comes in many colors and is readily available in craft and fabric stores. Pellon®, a heavy white fabric used for facings in sewing, is less known but just as useful in quilting and other student crafts. It's easy to cut and students can draw directly on it using markers or crayons. Also, because of its texture, Pellon® sticks to felt with no adhesive at all, so you can shift and replace your quilt blocks at leisure with no mess whatsoever!

Quilt It!

 1   Decide on a theme for your quilt and create a layout.

 2   Show students how easy it is to cut and draw on Pellon®. Draw on the material yourself and cut out a shape related to your theme. Show students that Pellon® is somewhat transparent, and can be used to trace shapes or objects from books.

 3   You can use one large piece of felt for your background, or you can have students make individual felt blocks that can be assembled into a whole. If you are using a large piece of felt as background, simulate quilt blocks by dividing the felt with ribbon. Either glue the ribbon in place or tack it onto a bulletin board on which you have hung the felt background. If students create individual felt quilt blocks, have them glue the felt onto a cardboard square for durability.

 4   Instruct students to create designs from Pellon® that fit your theme or their individual assignments.

 5   Have students attach their finished Pellon® artwork onto their quilt squares (if they have made them) or directly onto your large felt quilt background. Students can attach the Pellon® simply by pressing it onto the felt (if you want your quilt to be changeable) or by gluing it (for a permanent quilt).

See It in Action

Countries of the World Quilt (p. 40)

Vinyl Window Shade Quilt

Can you imagine your students' amazement when they create a quilt out of an ordinary window shade? The shade becomes the backing for the classroom quilt—ready to display the students' quilt blocks. Vinyl shades are inexpensive and often can be found at yard sales or thrift stores. Stores that cut shades to order sometimes will donate the discarded pieces.

Materials

- vinyl window shade
- vinyl glue or thumb tacks
- markers
- student art or writing related to the quilt's theme
- ribbon, yarn, or colored tape

Quilt It!

1. Obtain a vinyl window shade to use as your quilt background.

2. Decide on a theme for your quilt and create a layout, taking into account the size of your vinyl window shade.

3. Have students create artwork or writing projects to attach to the shade as quilt blocks.

4. Attach student work to the shade using vinyl glue. The student pieces can be separated into quilt blocks by using ribbon or yarn. The shade can be hung anywhere, and is easily transported, stored, and displayed.

See It in Action

Rain Poetry Quilt (p. 51)

Ribbon Quilt

he wide array of ribbons available offers yet another way of displaying student-made quilt blocks. Pieces of ribbon can be arranged vertically or horizontally against a background. Student work can then be glued or pinned to the ribbon. Another option is to weave the ribbon in and out of the quilt blocks, which are tacked to a bulletin board or cork strip.

Quilt It!

 1 Decide on a theme for your quilt and create a layout.

 2 Have students decorate their quilt squares.

 3 Tack or staple the ribbon to the bulletin board or cork strip.

 4 Pin or tape students' quilt squares on top of the ribbon to create a quilt-like effect. You can also attach the quilt squares directly to the background and thread the ribbon in and out of the quilt blocks.

See It in Action

Our State Quilt (p. 37)

Materials

- wide ribbons
- tacks, stapler, or tape
- bulletin board or cork strip
- quilt squares

Muffin Tin Quilt

A quilt from muffin tins? Sure! Just flip over the muffin tin to its backside, and you have six or 12 ready-made "blocks" just crying out to be decorated by students. Students can paint people, animals, or other creatures directly onto the tins or create round paper projects to be glued onto them.

Materials

- 6- or 12-cup muffin tins
- paints (if students are going to paint directly onto muffin tins) or paper (for artwork that will be pasted onto muffin tins)
- small nails or tacks
- yarn
- quilt background of your choosing
- bulletin board or other display board

Quilt It!

 1 Decide on a theme for your quilt and work with students to design a layout.

 2 Have students make artwork on small paper circles that can be glued onto the tins. Or, have students paint directly onto the tins. (Never have more than two students painting at one time. Twelve students painting on one small muffin tin is a recipe for chaos!)

 3 Using tacks or nails, attach the decorated muffin tin to the quilt background and the bulletin board. First, hang the background on the board. Then attach the muffin tin by pushing a tack or nail through the already-existing hole. (Most muffin tins have holes for hanging. If your tin does not, create a hole using a drill or a hammer and nail.)

See It in Action

Muffin Tin Calendar Quilt (p. 48)

Other Ideas

- Portraits of historical figures
- Snow people mounted on winter-theme fabric

Graduated Pages Quilt

These interactive quilts are constructed from graduated-pages books made by students. A graduated-pages book is made from a series of slightly overlapping pages (see p. 24). The outer margin of each page serves as a label or a clue to what is on the hidden part of the page. Graduated Pages Quilts offer students a fun way to reveal something of interest about themselves on each page. If you're doing a unit on plants or animals, have students use the pages to give clues about "mystery" animals or plants.

Quilt It!

 Decide on your quilt theme and your quilt background.

 Design a layout for your quilt. This will determine the size for your graduated-pages books.

 Have students make blank graduated-pages books by stapling together sheets of paper of increasing length (see p. 24).

 Work together with students to decide on the contents of the books, then assign each student (or team of students) a book to make.

 Attach the finished books to the background, then display your Graduated Pages Quilt.

(see p. 24)

Materials

- paper for graduated-pages books
- markers or other writing implements
- magazine pictures, photographs, or other illustrations
- stapler, tape, or glue

See It in Action

Colorful Language Quilt (p. 43)

Other Ideas

- Who Is This Politician? Mystery Quilt
- Who Is This Teacher? Mystery Quilt
- Who Is This Sports Figure? Mystery Quilt
- Where in the World? Geography Mystery Quilt

Making a Graduated Pages Book

Give each student five sheets of white paper. Help students staple the sheets together across the top. Have them cut one inch from the bottom of page 4, two inches from page 3, three inches from page 2, and four inches from the top page. The resulting book will have pages that are staggered, as shown.

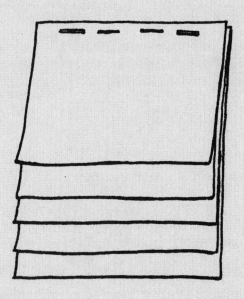

Floor or Tabletop Puzzle Quilt

This is essentially a quilt with no background. Students make quilt squares and then arrange them on a tabletop or floor. Students can piece the blocks together any way they please or any way you direct them. Students must work collaboratively to arrive at a pattern for the quilt. A quilt like this works well when you want students to see that pieces can be put together in different ways for a variety of purposes. For example, you can have students make quilt blocks depicting different types of birds, then arrange them by size, by habitat, or by color. You can also make a quilt that is a true puzzle by drawing blocks onto oaktag and cutting them apart into puzzle-like pieces.

Quilt It!

 Decide on a theme for your quilt.

 Give students oaktag or cardboard squares and have them illustrate or decorate them according to your theme. (Any material can be used for the blocks, but oaktag and cardboard are very durable. Due to the nature of this quilt, these blocks will have to endure a lot of student handling. If you have access to a laminator, you can use regular paper and laminate it before students begin assembling the quilt.)

Materials

■ oaktag or cardboard squares

■ supplies for decorating or illustrating the squares

■ floor or tabletop for display

■ large plastic bag for storage

3 Have students piece together the quilt on a floor or tabletop. Have them explore different ways of categorizing the blocks.

4 Store the blocks in a large plastic bag for later use.

See It in Action

Endangered Species Quilt (p. 52)

Other Ideas

- Minerals (arrange by color, formation type, or where found)
- Animals (arrange by size, animal classification, or whether they're carnivore, herbivore, or omnivore)

Fabric Quilt

If you can lay out and plan a paper quilt, you can do the same for a fabric quilt. Students can decorate fabric blocks using fabric crayons or paints. Don't have students piece together their blocks. Consider recruiting volunteers to help sew the individual blocks together, add batting, and back the quilt. There are also dozens of excellent books written especially for beginning quilters. It does take a lot of work to make a fabric quilt in the classroom, but it's well worth it! A fabric quilt with a block designed by each student in your class is a beautiful memento that will last a lifetime.

Materials

- paper for sketching the designs
- fabric for the quilt blocks, backing, and batting
- fabric markers or fabric paints
- thread and needles

Quilt It!

 1 Choose a theme for your quilt and create a layout. If you like, incorporate a lattice and a border.

 2 Explain to students that they will plan and practice their designs on paper before working on fabric.

 3 Once students' designs are finalized, have them draw them on plain fabric squares using fabric crayons, paints, or markers. Be sure that students leave space for sewing around the edges of their blocks. (Consult a basic quilting book or a master quilter to determine exactly how much space to leave.)

 4 A quilting bee can be planned if the quilt is to be constructed in the classroom, or a volunteer quilter can take the students' squares and complete the quilt at home. Sew loops of material at the top of the quilt for hanging.

See It in Action

Then and Now Quilt (p. 33); States of the Union Quilt (p. 38); Cinderella Quilt (p. 42)

Making It Happen:
Quilting Activities
Across the Curriculum

In this section, you will see how real students in real classrooms—in most cases, our classrooms—have brought to life the quilting formats from the previous section. For each quilt shown, we describe the inspiration, list the quilting format (with a page reference for instructions), and provide basic instructions. In some cases, we offer tips and variations. We hope you'll mesh these ideas with your own to create quilts that suit your students and your curriculum.

CLASSROOM COMMUNITY QUILTS

Getting-to-Know-You Quilt

The Idea

Getting to know each other! This quilt is a natural for the beginning of the school year. It introduces students to each other and to the idea of quilting as a cooperative classroom activity.

Format

Basic Quilt (p. 9) or
Plastic Bag Quilt (p. 11)

How It Works

Students make this quilt at the
beginning of the school year. Each
block is a mini autobiography,
including fun facts and a photo.

Tell students that they will be
making quilt blocks that tell the rest
of the class something important about
themselves. You can ask for specific
information to be included on the
quilt squares, or let students decide for
themselves what to include, such as:

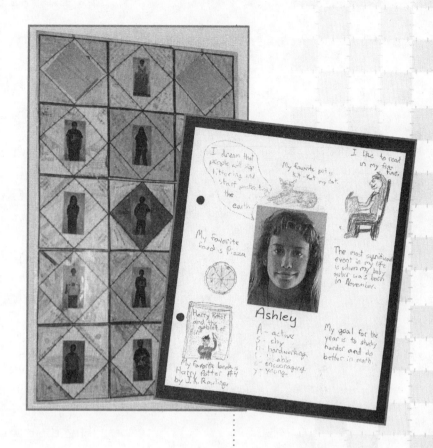

- hobbies
- goals for the year
- pet peeves
- favorite foods
- favorite books
- you'd never guess it, but I _____

The quilt blocks can also be designed as collages of students' lives,
using magazine photos as the raw material. Depending on how much
space you have, student names can be included in each student's block
or placed in adjoining blocks. Encourage kids to be creative with the
lettering. They can spell their names with glitter-sprinkled glue or letters
cut from newspaper or wrapping paper.

Variation

Have each student interview a classmate, then create a quilt block
describing that person.

Tips

The quilt can be
displayed in a
prominent place
throughout the
school year as a
tribute to students.
It can also be
featured at open
houses and during
American Education
Week (the week before
Thanksgiving), as a
way of introducing
class members to
parents and visitors
and as a means of
promoting class
community.

Random Acts of Kindness Quilt

Practice Random Acts of Kindness

A M S

Say something nice to someone.

The Idea

This quilt builds community and advances the cause of kindness in the classroom, inspired by the national "Random Acts of Kindness" movement.

Format

Basic Quilt (p. 9)

How It Works

The quilt shown here resulted from a monthlong social studies/literature unit on being kind and spreading kindness. The students conducted a school-wide kindness campaign, distributing posters, stickers, buttons, and good deeds around the school. Students created quilt squares describing their own acts of kindness. Joined together, the squares represented many different ways to show kindness.

To create a Random Acts of Kindness Quilt in your classroom, choose a way of thinking about kindness that best suits your curriculum and classroom community. Then, have students make appropriate quilt blocks. For example, students could make a block symbolizing the kindest thing anyone has ever done for them, or describing the way in which they themselves have been kind.

Piecing It Together Idea

Quilt Stationery

When you're undertaking any unit or activity, you can create quilt stationery to accompany it. Give students a blank quilt block and have them decorate it with the class theme in mind—kindness, plant life, or the Civil War, for example. Then use a photocopier to reduce the blocks. Place them around a sheet of paper to create a border, and photocopy as many copies as you need. The stationery can be used for published writing, invitations and thank-you notes to guest speakers, or simple note taking.

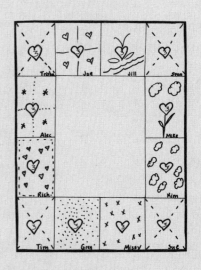

Memories Quilt

The Idea

Help students recall and commemorate the experiences they've had in your classroom with the Memories Quilt. This quilt is most appropriate for the end of the school year or at the mid-year break.

Format

Basic Quilt (p. 9)

How It Works

Reflect back over the school year with your students, reminding them of key events, such as field trips, parties, and books you've read as a class. Then have each student choose an event that was of special significance to him or her and depict it in a quilt block. The quilt shown here was created at the end of the school year by the third-

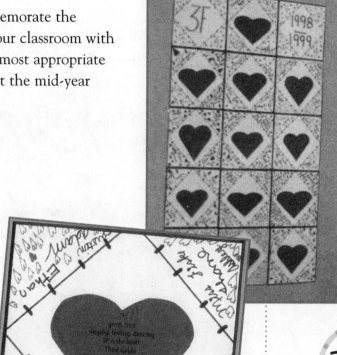

grade class of Alice Fiske, one of this book's authors. Each student wrote a memory on a heart, then had fellow students autograph the blank spaces around the square.

Variation

Give each student a copy of a class picture to decorate and use as the centerpiece for his or her square.

Tips

If your students make a memory quilt at the end of the school year, save it and show it to your new students the following September. Discussing the quilt can be a good lead-in activity to making a Getting-to-Know-You Quilt, and is also a fun way to get students excited about the activities and units you have planned for the coming year.

Penny Quilt

The Idea

This quilt incorporates pennies and historical information about the year each coin was minted.

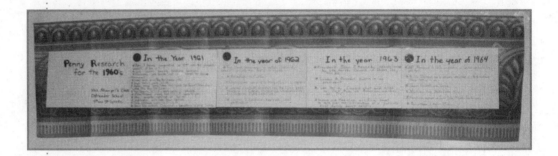

Format

Basic Quilt (p. 9), with wallpaper background

How It Works

Collect pennies with as many different mint dates as possible. Give each student a penny. Have students research the events that occurred in the year their coin was minted. Students can gather information online or through library resources, such as old newspapers and almanacs. Some ideas to research: most popular song, most popular kids' TV show, names of elected officials, biggest news event, and important weather events. Students can also focus on a particular aspect of history for their year—sports, politics, or overseas news, for example. Have students glue their coin to an index card, which will serve as your quilt block, and fill the rest of the card with facts and pictures related to the year the penny was minted. Glue the cards to a quilt background that fits your theme. Pictured above is a penny banner quilt using coins from the 1960s.

Variations

The Dollar Bill Quilt is a little more expensive than the Penny Quilt, but offers a fun way to teach United States geography. The quilt blocks can describe the location of the Federal Reserve Bank where the dollar was issued. (It's printed in the circle on the left-hand side of each bill front.) A cheaper alternative is a Quarter Quilt, using the new state quarters as they become available.

Book Link

The Hundred Penny Box by Sharon Bell Mathis (Viking Press, 1986) is an excellent penny-related book to share with students working on this project.

Olympics Quilt

The Idea

This quilt is inspired by the Olympic games, which happens every two years. This quilting project will help you turn this exciting event into a learning experience.

Format

Plastic Bag Quilt (p. 11)

How It Works

The plastic bag quilt shown was made by third-grade students from Cambridge Central School in New York, to commemorate the 2000 Summer Olympic Games in Sydney, Australia.

To make one in your classroom, decide which aspect of the Olympic Games you want to highlight. Depending on your curricular needs, you might choose to focus on the host country, the sports themselves, the athletes, or even the history of the Olympic Games. Have students research their topic, then use a combination of illustration, collage, and writing to create an appropriate quilt block. Use the Olympic rings or other sports theme to decorate the borders or extra blocks. If you're lucky enough to have an athlete from your hometown competing in the Olympics, dedicate the entire quilt to that person and send it to him or her.

Variation

Create a quilt commemorating a different sporting event, such as World Cup Soccer or the World Series.

Then and Now Quilt

The Idea

A quilt comparing today's prices with those of long ago—a topic that never ceases to fascinate kids—serves as a good entry point into a study of life in bygone eras.

Format

Fabric Quilt (p. 26)

How It Works

The students who made this quilt were shocked when they learned how little a candy cane cost during the early 1900s. They were inspired to continue their price-comparison research and create a quilt displaying their findings.

To create a similar quilt in your classroom, choose a date in history that is important in your curriculum, then select an item that students like and is small enough to be incorporated into a quilt, such as the candy canes on the quilt shown on page 33. Have students work in groups to find out how much the item costs today, and what its price was on the date you selected. Then, have them research the price of other things that interest them (and you), such as food, toys, books, transportation, or entertainment. Have each group create a quilt block incorporating the item and the prices they researched.

Primary Sources Quilt: The Toll Road

The Idea

To think like historians, students need to use historians' tools—primary documents, such as maps, journals, photos, newspaper accounts, and memorabilia. Quilting is an excellent way for students to display what they have learned after sifting through primary source documents.

Format

Basic Quilt (p. 9)

How It Works

Judy Russert's fourth-grade students made the quilt pictured here after studying maps and other original documents pertaining to the Erie Canal toll road. Students discussed the documents, then split up into groups to design and construct a quilt using the information they had gathered.

Each group designed a nine-patch quilt with blocks that included drawings of the toll collector, a vehicle that used the road, and alternative uses for the toll road. Each block had a border design and was glued to a larger piece of wallpaper. The blocks were then glued to a piece of plastic foam display board.

Variation

While studying about the United States government, students in Molly Oakley's fifth-grade class examined actual copies of the original U.S. Constitution—a primary document if ever there was one—and discussed the meaning of the Preamble. Then, teams of students illustrated various aspects of the Preamble. The original artwork was displayed in the corridor and Ms. Oakley shot photos of each illustration. From those photos, students constructed a quilt, shown at right.

Lighthouse Quilt

The Idea

Students study the construction, lore, and 2,000-year history of lighthouses, then create a quilt to display lighthouse models they build.

Format

Foam Tray Quilt (p. 15)

How It Works

In Judy Russert's fourth-grade class, students became fascinated by lighthouses after reading *Beacons of Light: Lighthouses* by Gail Gibbons (William Morrow, 1990). Each student went on to research and write a report on a particular lighthouse in the United States. Next, students built models of their lighthouses using construction paper, bubble wrap, sand, markers, and paint. The models were mounted on recycled plastic foam trays and arranged in a quilt-like fashion on a piece of sea-blue fabric.

Variation

Create a Ship Quilt to complement the Lighthouse Quilt. Feature the types of ships that would have plied the waters around the structures in the Lighthouse Quilt.

Biographical Time Line Quilt

The Idea

Made up of blocks that symbolize the events in a person's life, this quilt lends itself to historical figures and current world leaders. But it's certainly not limited to that. Students can portray the life of one of their ancestors, their favorite pop star, themselves, or even their teacher!

Formats

Plastic Bag Quilt (p. 11) and Basic Quilt (p. 9), on wallpaper background

How It Works

Choose a person you are studying in class and, with students' help, choose a series of events in that person's life. Have each student design a quilt block representing one of the events. If you wind up with more students than events, have some students work on blocks for the quilt's perimeter—lettering for the person's name or the person's portrait, for example. The Grandma Moses Plastic Bag Quilt pictured above was made by third graders after they studied the famous folk artist. They recorded key events from Grandma Moses's life onto quilt blocks, inserted the blocks into plastic bags, then arranged them in chronological order to create the quilt.

The quilt banners pictured below commemorate the lives of Amelia Earhart and Eleanor Roosevelt. Both quilts have wallpaper backgrounds.

News Quilt

The Idea

This ever-changing quilt highlights events in the news—a patchwork of world affairs.

Format

Plastic Bag Quilt (p. 11), on a newspaper background

How It Works

To create the background, cover a posterboard or plastic foam display board with newspaper pages. Attach quart-sized self-sealing plastic bags to the background, leaving spaces between each bag. Have students make labels for each bag indicating the news categories you want to include, such as local, national, world or international, sports, or science. To create contrast between the quilt blocks and the background, place plain sheets of paper or oaktag in each bag. Create a news-quilt schedule for the class in which you assign students to periodically bring in articles that fit into each of the categories. You can change the quilt daily, weekly, or monthly.

Variation

Create a news quilt for a historical era you are studying, such as an Ancient Roman news quilt or a Colonial America news quilt. Have students work in teams to write stories and headlines for each category. (Examples: "Julius Caesar Murdered!" or "Eli Whitney Invents Amazing Contraption!") Be creative with the decorative borders and make them fit your era.

Our State Quilt

The Idea

In many states, study of state history is an important part of the social studies curriculum. Students' knowledge of their state's rich story and culture can be displayed beautifully in a quilt.

Formats
Plastic Bag Quilt (p. 11) and Ribbon Quilt (p. 21)

How It Works
The wallpaper plastic-bag quilt shown here was made by Jean Mumper's fourth and fifth graders to display what they had learned during an exploration of the economy, population, environment, and topography of the regions of New York. Create a similar quilt for your state, or have students focus their research on different areas. You can also display fun facts about your state in a ribbon quilt.

The second quilt shown here was made by the same group of fourth and fifth graders in New York (a group of avid quilters). Each student was assigned a letter of the alphabet, found an aspect of the state with that initial letter, then illustrated it in a quilt block. For example, A is for Albany, B is for Brooklyn Bridge, C is for Central Park, and so on. The quilt blocks were glued to heavy strips of cardboard, threaded together with ribbon, and displayed on a bulletin board. Blocks with pictures of apples (since New York City is known as "The Big Apple") were interspersed with student illustrations.

States of the Union Quilt

The Idea
Students become familiar with the shapes of the states and the locations of their capitals as they create a traditional fabric quilt depicting the 50 states.

Format
Fabric Quilt (p. 26)

How It Works
In the quilt shown here, fifth-grade students cut out a fabric shape for each of the 50 states. They stitched each shape onto a cloth quilt block using embroidery stitches, such as the cross-stitch and running stitch. Students sewed buttons to each state to indicate the state capital. If you like this idea but don't trust your students' sewing skills (or yours!), replicate the quilt using paper and glue instead of fabric and thread.

Variation

Instead of a States of the Union Quilt, make a Nations of the World Quilt.

Postcard and Map Quilt

The Idea

By creating a quilt from postcards, students get to know about the landmarks and history of a distant place.

Format

Artifact Quilt (p. 12), on posterboard background

How It Works

Decide what place or region you want to focus on for this quilt, then find a source for the postcards! To obtain cards, encourage the class to write to tourist bureaus, adopt a sister school in another part of the country or world, or have postcards sent to you by community members who travel to other areas. Once you have your postcards, get a map of the area you've chosen.

In the Washington, D.C., postcard quilt shown here, postcards were attached around the edges of a posterboard with a map in the middle. Each card is edged with stitching lines—drawn with markers—to create a quilt-like look. You can use yarn or string to link each postcard to its location on the map. You can also use the map as a background instead of the quilt's centerpiece.

World Traveler Suitcase Quilt

The Idea

A suitcase-shaped quilt and a more traditionally shaped quilt give students a fun way to display what they learn during a study of the continents or any geographic region.

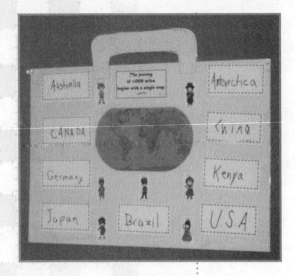

Format

Unique!

How It Works

The suitcase quilt shown here was part of Alice Fiske's third-grade class project in which students "traveled" to different parts of the world through the Internet, books, and videos during their social studies class. To make the suitcase, students cut two 12- by 18-inch pieces of oaktag in the shape of a suitcase and taped them together. They designed the outside with straps, buckles, zippers, and a nametag to look like luggage. They also used Velcro® to simulate hinges so that students can close their suitcases while "traveling." As students completed their "visits" to each country, they added pictures and stickers (similar to those available in tourist stores) of the places they visited to their suitcases.

Countries of the World Quilt

The Idea

Make this class quilt to complement the World Traveler Suitcase Quilt above, or to enhance any geography unit.

Format

Pellon® and Felt Quilt (p. 18)

How It Works

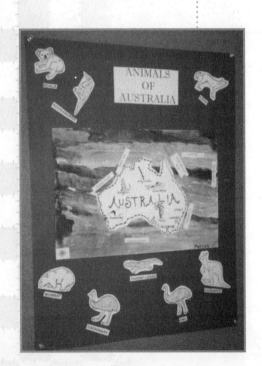

During your study of the continents or countries of the world, have students decide as a group which country interests them most—the way real world travelers might sit down and talk about which part of the world they most enjoy visiting. Then, make a class quilt showcasing that country, like the Australia quilt shown here. The map of Australia and illustrations of animals are made from Pellon® and are attached to blue felt to represent the water surrounding Australia.

Idiom Quilt

The Idea

Students love to play with language and are fascinated by puns, riddles, and jokes. This quilt will bring out students' playful side, while hammering home the concept of idioms.

Format

Paper Frame Quilt (p. 17)

How It Works

To make this quilt, students drew funny illustrations that literally interpreted well-known idioms from the English language. Then, they placed the illustrations in paper frames and assembled the frames into a quilt.

To begin such a project in your classroom, explain to students that idioms are figures of speech that make little sense when interpreted literally. For example, "raining cats and dogs," "on the nose," and "hit the hay." Discuss with students why idioms often present difficulties for people learning English as a second language. Then, have students brainstorm a list of idioms. Some idioms they might know are:

- stick your neck out
- under the weather
- fly off the handle
- on pins and needles
- cat got your tongue

- break the ice
- nose to the grindstone
- head in the sand
- hold your horses

Have each student choose an idiom to illustrate on a quilt block. If you like, have students include a caption on the quilt block in which they use the idiom in a sentence.

Variation

Invite students to create a Proverbs Quilt by illustrating proverbs (such as "The early bird catches the worm," or "Curiosity killed the cat") on quilt blocks.

Book Link

The Scholastic Dictionary of Idioms by Marvin Terban (Scholastic, 1996) is a fascinating book that explains the origins of hundreds of idioms in the English language. Students will love this fun fact-filled book!

Cinderella Quilt

The Idea

It's amazing to see how the same basic story appears in folktales from around the world. It makes one realize that we are all part of one big family. Students find it fascinating to compare the way a single story is told in different cultures, and there is no better way than quilting for students to show their understanding of different cultures' tales.

Format

Fabric Quilt (p. 26)

How It Works

Versions of "Cinderella" are told in cultures all around the globe, and many of those versions have been published as children's books. As a result, Cinderella is an ideal story for a cross-cultural study of folktales. It's also wonderful to culminate such a study by making a class quilt, such as the one pictured above.

To get started, ask students what they consider to be the main events in "Cinderella." Then share with them some of the books at left—Cinderella variants from different cultures. Talk about the similarities and differences among the tales. Then have students make quilt blocks depicting each version you have read together.

The students who made the quilt pictured above read many variants of "Cinderella" and also studied the countries where the versions originated.

Book Links

The Egyptian Cinderella by Shirley Climo (Egypt)

Fair, Brown, & Trembling: An Irish Cinderella Story by Jude Daly (Ireland)

Moss Gown by W. Hooks (United States)

Chinye by Obi Onyefulu (West Africa)

Mufaro's Beautiful Daughters by John Steptoe (Africa)

Baba Yaga and Vasilisa the Brave by Marianna Mayer (Russia)

Poetry Quilt

The Idea

Poetry can be displayed using almost any quilting format. The challenge is to choose a quilt format that best complements the poetry. Use the quilts here as inspiration for similar projects in your classroom.

Formats

Basic Quilt (p. 9), Paper Plate Quilt (p. 16), and Graduated Pages Quilt (p. 23)

How It Works

Shape Poetry Quilt

Students wrote their own poems inspired by various shapes (such as a leaf, animal, or car). The poems were mounted on paper and arranged on a generic background to resemble a quilt.

Acrostic Poetry Quilt

Each line in an acrostic poem begins with each successive letter of a word or name. Here's an acrostic poem using the name Adam:

Always on his skateboard

Daredevil, flying high

Aaaarrgggh! Hurtling to the ground! Crash!

Maybe a little less daring next time

Illustrated acrostic poems can be arranged to form a quilt. The quilt pictured here was made by students in Terry Hewson's third-grade class. Each student drew a self-portrait on a paper plate and wrote an acrostic poem about himself or herself.

Colorful Language Quilt

If you're sad, you have the "blues." If you're jealous, you're "green" with envy. Colors evoke many feelings and interpretations, making them a great subject for poetry. They're visual, too,

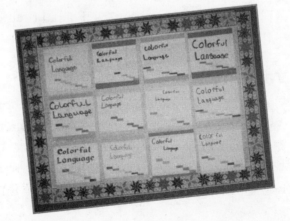

which makes them a fabulous subject for quilting. The graduated pages quilt shown here was made by fifth-grade students who had discussed the relationship between color, mood, and feelings. The border for each page of each book was made from a paint chip of a different color. On the hidden part of each page, students wrote poems about the color on the border.

Book Link

Hailstones and Halibut Bones by Mary O'Neill (Doubleday, 1990) is a renowned book of poetry about the colors of the spectrum.

Literature Response Quilt

The Idea

Quilts are great for showcasing students' responses to books. Creating a quilt related to a book about quilting is a natural, but it's just as easy to make a quilt about any literature.

Formats

Basic Quilt (p. 9) and Plastic Bag Quilt (p. 11)

How It Works

The basic quilt shown on top was made by students who had read and enjoyed the nonfiction book *Somewhere Today* by Bert Kitchen (Candlewick Press, 1994), which features stunning full-page portraits of animals in action. The book captures the wonder of the natural world, as does this student quilt.

The second quilt pictured here was made by students in Teddy Harrington's third-grade class after they had read *The Keeping Quilt* by Patricia Polacco (Aladdin, 2001). The beautifully illustrated book tells the true story of a quilt, made from bits of old clothes, that has been handed down from generation to generation in the author's family. In response to the book, Ms. Harrington's students made plastic bag quilt blocks that symbolized their own family histories and traditions.

Variations

Students can illustrate and assemble a fictional geography quilt featuring various celestial locations visited by characters from *A Wrinkle in Time* by Madeline L'Engle (Farrar Strauss & Giroux, 1990). They can also create a Harry Potter time-line quilt with blocks representing key events in the young wizard's life.

Word Collage Quilt

The Idea

Just as fabrics make up quilts, words make up whole ideas through sentences, paragraphs, and stories. A Word Collage Quilt celebrates the beauty of language.

Format

Basic Quilt (p. 9), on a bulletin board

How It Works

A third-grade class made the quilt shown here after reading *Donavan's Word Jar* by Monalisa DeGross (HarperCollins, 1994), a delightful chapter book about a boy who discovers the joy of collecting and sharing words. First, the third graders began collecting words of their own. A large jar was placed in an accessible spot, along with slips of paper and pencils. Students were invited to add to the jar by jotting a new word on a slip of paper and dropping it in the jar. Occasionally, students were asked to add words that relate to a unit the class was studying. After a few months, each student randomly picked a dozen words from the jar. The words brought back fond memories of things the class had shared, units of study, and individual favorite words. The students then took their words and used them to outline a jar in the middle of a square quilt block.

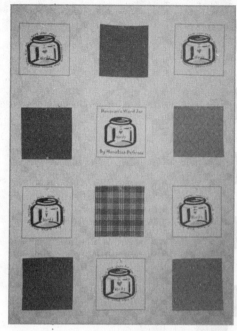

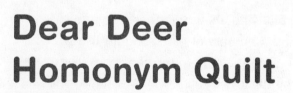

Dear Deer Homonym Quilt

The Idea

The English language provides many opportunities for playful interpretation and enjoyment. Just look at the popularity of the Amelia Bedelia book series, whose main character has a real knack for misinterpreting the English language! The quilt pictured here was inspired by a playful homonym pair—dear deer—that fit perfectly with December, the month in which it was created.

Format

Basic Quilt (p. 9)

How It Works

This quilt was made as part of a homonyms unit. To make the reindeer, students started with a brown triangle, which they glued into the quilt square template. One side of the triangle formed the top of the reindeer's head, and the point opposite it was its nose. Next, students cut out antlers and ears from scraps of paper and glued them to the square. They drew faces on the deer with crayons and markers, and glued red pom-poms to form the noses. Wiggly eyes brought the quilt squares to life. To reinforce the concept of the "dear" part of the homonym, students drew hearts in the corners. They decorated the borders with "stitching" lines to simulate quilting.

Variations

Students can also create a Hoarse Horse Quilt, a New Gnu Quilt, or a quilt made up of blocks that each represent a different homonym pair.

(MATH AND SCIENCE QUILTS)

Fractions Quilt

The Idea

Quilts are really all about fractions—dividing a whole into a number of parts. A quilt using fractions as the motif can help turn fractions from drudgery into a thing of beauty.

Format

Basic Quilt (p. 9)

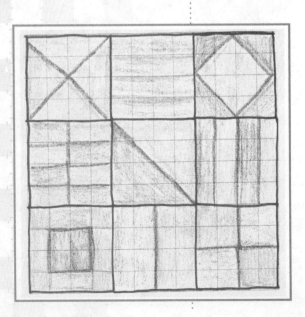

How It Works

While constructing the squares for the quilt shown, class members discussed how fractions are important in real life—in cooking, measuring, sewing, building, and dividing things between friends!

To make the quilt, students were given grid paper cut into squares. They then drew thick lines to divide each square into nine equal sections. Each section was then divided and colored to represent different fractions.

Geometric Shapes Quilt

The Idea

Students design their own quilt blocks that incorporate geometric shapes they are studying in class.

Format

Basic Quilt (p. 9)

How It Works

The students who made this quilt were given a two-inch square of paper, and asked to cut it in half diagonally or straight

across. (Students ended up with either two triangles or two rectangles.) They then cut the halves in half, creating four triangles or four squares. Next, they were given a four-inch square of paper with a contrasting color. Each student designed a single quilt block by arranging his or her four smaller pieces on the larger square. The students were amazed at how many variations they designed.

Book Links

Fraction Action by Loreen Leedy (Scott Foresman, 1996) and *The Hershey's Milk Chocolate Fractions Book* by Jerry Pallotta and Rob Bolster (Cartwheel, 1999) are excellent fraction-related resources.

Muffin Tin Calendar Quilt

The Idea

If you're looking for new ways to teach the months of the year or history of the calendar, try making a calendar quilt from a 12-cup muffin tin.

Format

Muffin Tin Quilt (p. 22)

How It Works

Use this quilt as a supplement to lessons about the seasons, history of the calendar, different types of calendars, the pattern calendars follow, or the way calendars are set up.

For the quilt shown here, students decided on appropriate symbols for each of the 12 months of the year, then illustrated them on circular pieces of paper. The circles were laminated for durability before being glued to the muffin tin. Calendar pages for each month were hung below the muffin tin quilt. You can generate calendar pages on the computer, purchase them, or have students make them.

Math in Our Lives Quilt

The Idea

Often, students see mathematics as a topic that is studied in schools—not as something that has use in "real life." Create a quilt that will remind students of math's interesting and practical applications.

Format

Basic Quilt (p. 9)

How It Works

Get students in a math mood by reading math-related books (see Book Links, p. 49).

Brainstorm with students ways in which math is necessary for our survival and convenience. Students may mention telling time, following a schedule, noting page numbers in books, keeping score in sports, counting money, lining up in two's, or dividing a cake equally.

To make a quilt, such as the one on page 48, give students photocopies of the "Triangle in the Corners" quilt block pattern (p. 60). Have them use words and pictures to design blocks symbolizing how math is important in their lives.

Earth Day Quilt

The Idea

Concerns about the environment gave birth to Earth Day on April 22, 1970. More than 20 million people participated in the first Earth Day, and today it is celebrated all over the world. Earth Day has assumed a place in the curriculum and an Earth Day Quilt depicting ways students can honor and protect the earth is a great way to get your students thinking about the environment and their role in preserving it.

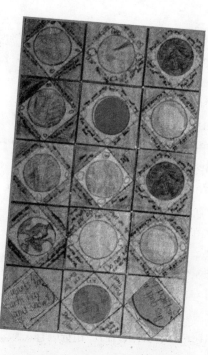

Format

Basic Quilt (p. 9)

How It Works

To create a quilt like the one shown above, give students photocopies of the "Diamond in the Middle" quilt block pattern (p. 57). Have each student draw his or her own version of the earth in the center of the block. In the corners, have them write tips for helping or saving the earth. The third graders who made this quilt used markers to draw small stitch-like hearts around their pictures of Earth.

Book Links

Measuring Penny by Loreen Leedy (Henry Holt, 2000)

Two Greedy Bears by Mirra Ginsburg (Aladdin, 1998)

The Kids' Money Book by Neale Godfrey (Scholastic, 1992)

The Greedy Triangle by Marilyn Burns (Pearson Learning, 1995)

Anno's Math Games by Mitsumasa Anno (Philomel, 1989)

Pigs on a Blanket by Amy Axelrod (Aladdin, 1998)

The Rajah's Rice by David Barry (W.H. Freeman, 1994)

Is a Blue Whale the Biggest Thing There Is? by Robert Wells (Scott Foresman, 1993)

The ABCs of Rocks and Minerals Quilt

The Idea

Many traditional quilt patterns, such as the Bear's Paw, Tulip Time, and Flying Geese, were inspired by nature. This quilt, which uses the alphabet to showcase students' knowledge of geology, takes that tradition a step further.

Format

Plastic Bag Quilt (p. 11)

How It Works

Tell students that they are going to make an Alphabet Rocks and Minerals Quilt. For inspiration, show them one or more of the books at left. They use the alphabet to present information about science and nature.

Next, assign each student a letter (or two letters, if you have a small class). Have each student choose a rock, mineral, or geological concept that begins with his or her assigned letter. You can follow the quilt design pictured here, with the letter in the upper left-hand corner, or come up with your own.

Rain Poetry Quilt

The Idea

Poetry about rain becomes the raw material for a vinyl window shade quilt.

Format

Vinyl Window Shade Quilt (p. 20)

How It Works

After students completed a unit about the weather, they each wrote poems about rain. These poems were attached to a window shade and hung outside the classroom for all to enjoy. The poems were affixed using double-faced tape, so they can be removed in the future, and the shade used for another purpose.

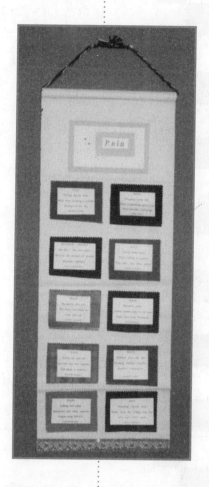

Foliage Photograph Quilt

The Idea

Nature photographs always seem like a great idea when you're shooting them. But what do you do with them afterward? This quilt is an inspired answer to that question.

Format

Artifact Quilt (p. 12)

How It Works

This quilt was made by a group of fifth-grade students studying leaves as part of a unit on plants. They went on a nature walk and, following tips given by an art teacher, shot photos of as many different types of leaves as they could. Students had the photos developed, then wrote poems about their leaf pictures. The photos and poems were displayed together as a quilt in the hallway outside their classroom.

Endangered Species Quilt

The Idea

An envelope quilt is the perfect way to present information about endangered animals. The quilt's viewer must work a little to find information about the species, just as we humans must work to understand the importance of the web of life on Earth.

Format

Envelope Quilt (p. 13) and Floor Puzzle Quilt (p. 25)

How It Works

The quilt pictured here was made by students who had just completed a unit on endangered species. Each student made an envelope and decorated the side that faces out with a picture of an endangered animal. Inside the envelopes students placed information about the animals pictured on the outside. You may want to make an envelope quilt before you begin a unit of study, so that students can place new information in the envelopes as they learn it.

Variation

Of course, an endangered species project can be depicted using almost any quilt format. Pictured below is a floor puzzle version (p. 25). Each block features a student-written acrostic poem about an endangered animal.

Food Label Mystery Quilt

The Idea

Get kids excited about nutrition by turning a bunch of food labels into a quilt-based guessing game.

Format

Artifact Quilt (p. 12)

How It Works

Have students bring in food labels from home. First, discuss with students how to read a food label. Then, remove anything that identifies the product that the label comes from. Arrange the labels to form a quilt, using a food-related background if you have one available. Make an answer key for the quilt that students can consult after they have tried to identify the food that each label comes from. If possible, display the quilt in your school cafeteria and get the whole student body involved in the guessing game.

Variation

Another nutrition-related quilt is the Food Pyramid Quilt below. Students brought in pictures of foods and placed them on the proper tier of the USDA (United States Department of Agriculture) Food Guide Pyramid.

Resources

For Students

Anderson, Janet. *Sunflower Sal*. New York: Whitman, 1997. Sunflower Sal has difficulty sewing quilts, but finds joy in planting farmland quilt scenes.

Atkins, Jeannine. *A Name on the Quilt: A Story of Remembrance*. New York: Atheneum, 1999. A young girl works on a panel for the AIDS quilt in loving memory of her uncle.

Avery, Kristin. *Crazy Quilt*. Glenview, Ill.: GoodYearBooks, 1994. A small bear takes a favorite piece of clothing from members of her family and creates a crazy quilt.

Beaty, Patricia. *O the Red Rose Tree*. New York: Morrow, 1994. In 1893, four young girls befriend an elderly woman and help locate seven shades of red for a special quilt she wants to make.

Bolton, Janet. *My Grandmother's Patchwork Quilt: A Book and Pocketful of Patchwork Pieces*. New York: Doubleday, 1994. Alternating pages describe a young girl's life on a farm and how she constructed a quilt to capture memories of her farm life.

Brumbeau, Jeff. *The Quiltmaker's Gift*. Duluth, Minn.: Pfeifer-Hamilton Publishers, 2000. A generous quiltmaker agrees to make a quilt for a greedy king under certain conditions, which cause the king to undergo a change of heart.

Edelman, Marian Wright. *Stand for Children*. New York: Hyperion Books for Children, 1998. A version of the speech delivered at a rally at the Lincoln Memorial is illustrated with multilayered quilts.

Edwards, Pamela Duncan. *Barefoot: Escape on the Underground Railroad*. New York: HarperCollins, 1997. A group of animals helps a runaway slave escape his pursuers. A quilt hung outside a cabin lets the slave know that it is a safe house.

Flournoy, Valerie. *The Patchwork Quilt*. New York: Dial, 1985. Using scraps cut from the family's old clothing, a young girl helps her grandmother and mother make a quilt that tells the story of her family's life.

Fowler, Christine. *Shota and the Star Quilt*. New York: Zero to Ten Ltd., 1998. Set in Minneapolis, this modern story examines one of the age-old themes—the triumph of love and friendship over power and greed.

Grifalconi, Ann. *Osa's Pride*. Boston: Little, Brown, 1990. Osa's grandmother tells her a story about the sins of pride and helps Osa gain a better perspective on things that really matter.

Guback, Georgia. *Luka's Quilt*. New York: Greenwillow Books, 1994. Luka is initially disappointed in the quilt her grandmother made for her, but eventually the two settle their differences.

Hopkinson, Deborah. *Sweet Clara and the Freedom Quilt*. New York: Knopf, 1993. A young slave stitches a quilt with a map pattern that guides her to freedom.

Kurtz, Shirley. *The Boy and the Quilt*. Intercourse, Pa.: Good Books, 1991. With help from his mother and sister, a little boy makes a quilt of his own.

Kuskin, Karla. *Patchwork Island*. New York: HarperCollins, 1994. A mother stitches the topography of their beautiful island into a quilt she is making for her child.

Levitin, Sonia. *A Piece of Home*. New York: Dial, 1996. A little boy moves from Russia and takes along his great-grandmother's special blanket.

Love, Anne. *Bess's Log Cabin Quilt*. New York: Holiday House, 1995. With her father away and her mother ill, a young girl works hard making a log-cabin quilt to save the family farm.

Lowe, Alice. *The Quilted Elephant and the Green Velvet Dragon*. New York: Simon & Schuster, 1991. Two of Andy's favorite stuffed animals face a crisis during a sleepover at a friend's house.

Lyons, Mary. *Stitching Stars: The Story Quilts of Harriet Powers*. New York: Charles Scribner's Sons, 1993. Quilts of family history, Bible stories, and folktales are featured in this biography of an African-American quilter.

McGill, Alice. *In the Hollow of Your Hand—Slave Lullabies*. Boston: Houghton Mifflin, 2000. A collection of lullabies by African slaves, accompanied with vibrant quilt collages and a CD, reveals hardships and sorrows as well as hope for better times to come.

Parton, Dolly. *Coat of Many Colors*. New York: HarperCollins, 1994. A poor girl cherishes her coat of many colors, made from rags by her mother, because the coat was made with love.

Paul, Ann. *Eight Hands Round: A Patchwork Alphabet*. New York: HarperCollins, 1991. This book introduces the letters of the alphabet with names of early American patchwork quilt patterns and explains the origins of the designs.

Polacco, Patricia. *The Keeping Quilt*. New York: Simon & Schuster, 1988. A homemade quilt ties together the lives of four generations of an immigrant Jewish family.

Ringgold, Faith. *Tar Beach*. New York: Crown Publishers, 1991. Based on the author's quilt painting, this story tells about a young girl who dreams of flying above her Harlem home.

Shea, Pegi. *The Whispering Cloth, A Refugee's Story*. Honesdale, Pa.: Boyds Mills Press, 1995. A young girl in a Thai refugee camp finds the story within herself to create her own pa'ndau.

Willard, Nancy. *The Mountains of Quilt*. San Diego, Calif.: Harcourt Brace Jovanovich, 1987. Four magicians lose their magic carpet, which eventually finds its way into the center of grandmother's quilt.

Willing, Karen Bates, and Julie Bates Dock. *Quilting Now and Then*. Ashland, Ore.: Now and Then Publications, 1994. A mother explains to her children how she quilts today and how the pioneers sewed long ago.

Xiong, Blia. *Nine-in-One, Grr! Grr! A Folktale from the Hmong People of Laos*. San Francisco: Children's Book Press, 1989. When the great god Shao promised Tiger nine cubs each year, Bird comes up with a clever trick to keep the land from being overrun by tigers. Illustrations depict the appliqué story cloths of the Hmong people.

Yorinks, Arthur. *The Alphabet Atlas*. Hong Kong: Winslow Press, 1999. In this alphabet book, 26 areas of the world are introduced using beautiful hand quilts.

Zerner, Amy, and Jessie Spicer Zerner. *The Dream Quilt*. Boston: Charles Tuttle, 1995. A boy has a series of adventures after touching the patches of a magic quilt.

For Teachers

Baycura, Debra. *Patchwork Math 1* and *Patchwork Math 2*. New York: Scholastic, 1990.

Bonica, Diane, and Kathy Devlin. *Cooperative Quilts: Classroom Quilts for the Entire School Year*. Torrance, Calif.: Fearon Teacher Aids, 1997.

Brunetto, Carolyn Ford. *Math Art Projects and Activities*. New York: Scholastic, 1997.

Buchberg, Wendy. *Quilting Activities Across the Curriculum*. New York: Scholastic, 1996.

Cigrand, Mariann, and Phyllis Howard. *Easy Literature-Based Quilts Around the Year*. New York: Scholastic, 2000.

King, Rendy, and Maureen King. *Quilt Connections*. Greensboro, N.C.: Carson-Dellosa, 1995.

Pike, Kathy, and Jean Mumper. *Books Don't Have to Be Flat! Innovative Ways to Publish Students' Writing in Every Curriculum Area*. New York: Scholastic, 1998.

Pike, Kathy, Jean Mumper, and Alice Fiske. *Teaching Kids to Care and Cooperate: 50 Easy Writing, Discussion & Art Activities That Help Develop Responsibility & Respect for Others*. New York: Scholastic, 2000.

Quiltmakers of Georgia. *The Olympic Games Quilts*. Birmingham, Ala.: Oxmoor House, Inc., 1996.

Zimmerman, Susan. *Quilts: A Thematic Unit*. Huntington Beach, Calif.: Teacher Created Materials, 1996.

QUILT BLOCK PATTERN
X through a Square

Quick Quilts Across the Curriculum Scholastic Professional Books

Diamond in the Middle

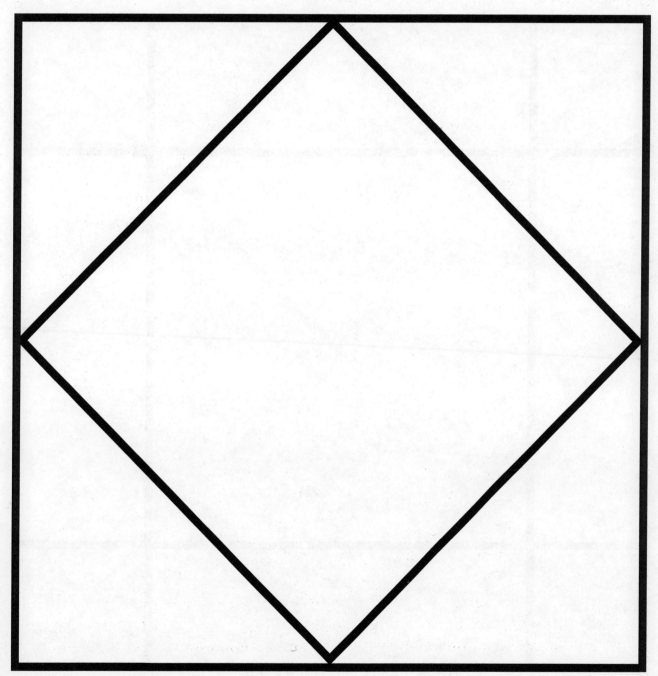

Crossed Corners

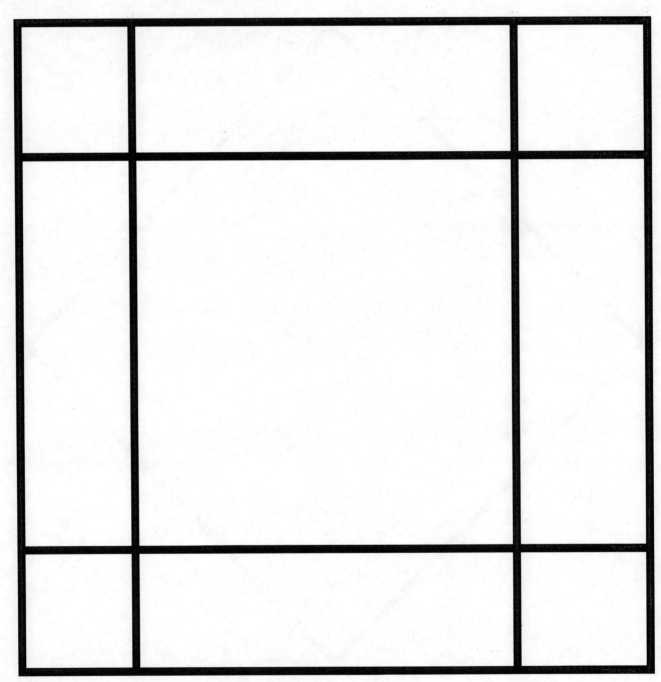

Quick Quilts Across the Curriculum Scholastic Professional Books

Squares in the Corners

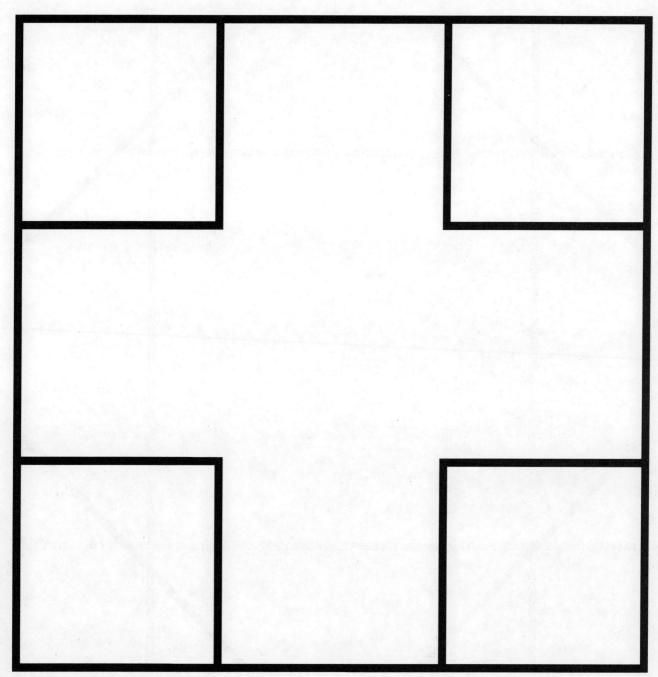

Quick Quilts Across the Curriculum Scholastic Professional Books

Triangle in the Corners

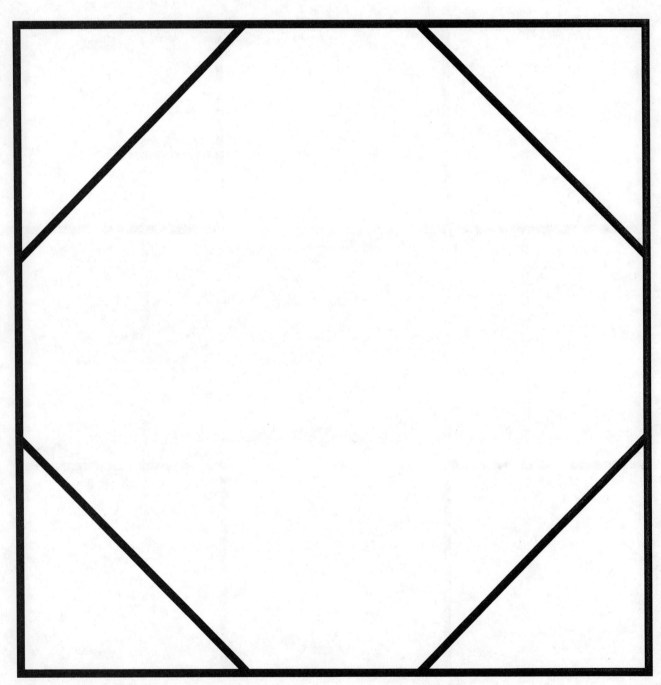

Quick Quilts Across the Curriculum Scholastic Professional Books

Open Frame Square

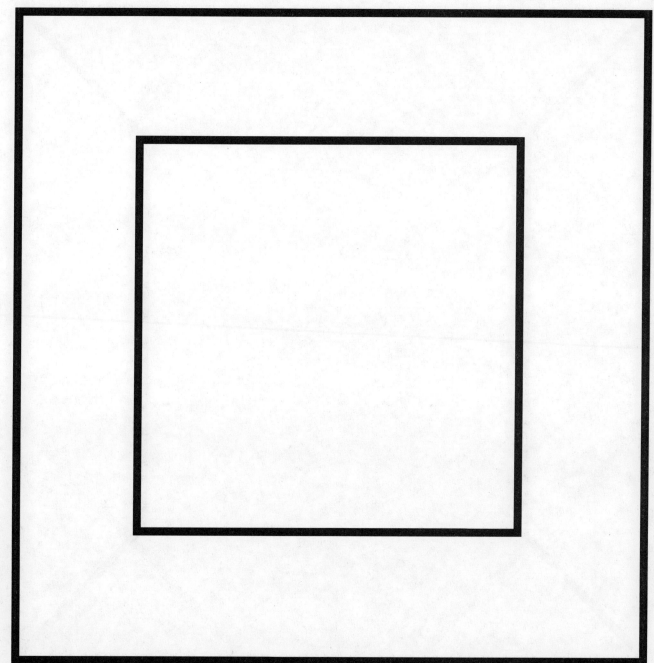

Quick Quilts Across the Curriculum Scholastic Professional Books

QUILT BLOCK PATTERN
Picture Frame

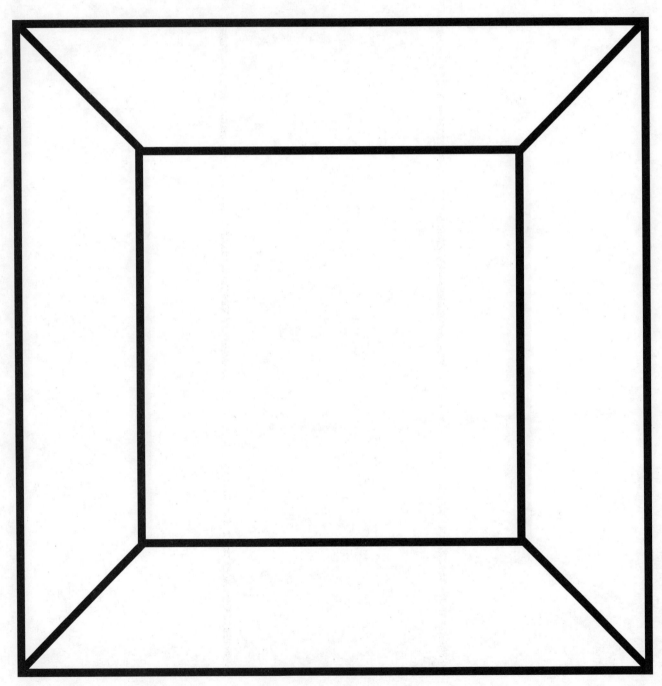

Quick Quilts Across the Curriculum Scholastic Professional Books

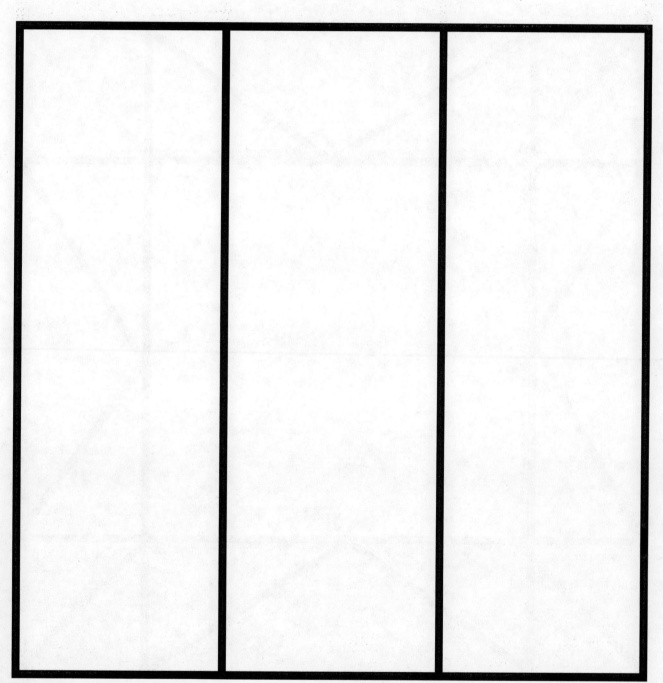

Quick Quilts Across the Curriculum Scholastic Professional Books

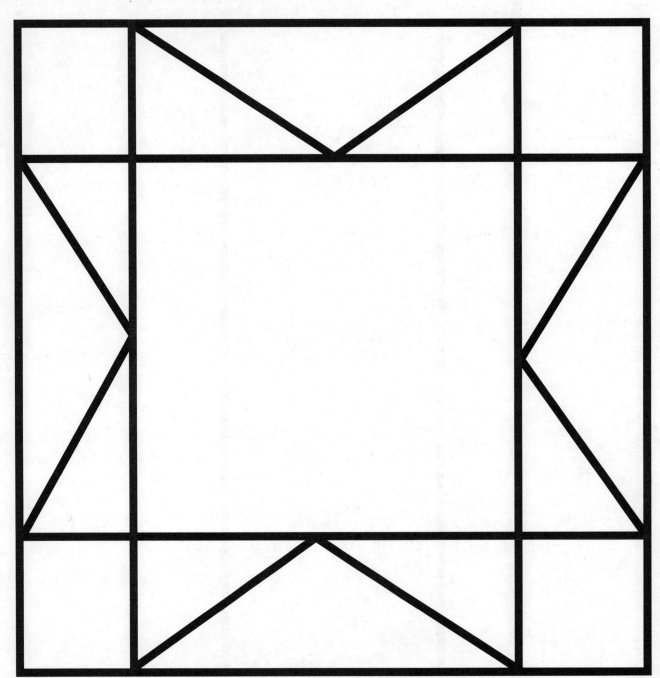

Quick Quilts Across the Curriculum Scholastic Professional Books